GW01150416

THE WHISPERS SERIES

THIS IS FOR YOU, DAD!

Compiled and edited by Lee Millam

Illustrations by Louise Barton

Nightingale
An imprint of Wimbledon Publishing Company
LONDON

Copyright © 2000
Illustrations © 2000

First published in Great Britain in 2000
by Wimbledon Publishing Company Ltd
P.O. Box 9779 London SW19 7ZG
All rights reserved

First published 2000 in Great Britain

ISBN: 1903222 23 0

Produced in Great Britain
Printed and bound in Hungary

The role of Mum always seems to be talked about more than Dad's, but despite what emphasis society has placed on the role of each parent, children love them equally. What is clear from this book is that children, no matter what their age, have a very special bond with their dads. He's the one who traditionally goes out each day and earns money for the family, looks after the garden, the DIY and the car, and still has time to play games, cuddle, encourage and read a bed time story.

For the many children who contributed their thoughts and feelings to this book, Dad is more than just a breadwinner. He's embarrassing, old-fashioned, annoying, inspiring, handsome, funny, but above all, loving.

Lee Millam
2000

Appearance

'His hair sticks up at the back and there is nothing that can flatten it, not even gel.'

Jane, 11

'He's dyed his hair blonde. It looks weird, there are streaks in it.'

Jamie, 12

'The bathroom has water on the floor and a dark ring around the bath after Dad's been in there. I wish he would try cleaning the bath - he spends hours in it.'

Sue, 17

'He sits watching the TV and starts picking the fluff out of his belly button. And he doesn't even bother to put it in the bin.'

Ruth, 12

'The sandals he likes to wear in the summer are embarrassing, especially because he wears them with socks.'

Jamie, 12

'He has hair coming out of his ears and nose, which he trims with a little machine every week.'

Ruth, 12

'I would change the size of him. He's got a very big belly.'

Alistair, 11

'He's got very big feet, which are very smelly.'

Ruth, 12

'I would change his hair cut - it's very short. He looks like a bald guy.'

Daniel, 12

'His clothes are outrageous. He's really got no fashion sense.'

Paul, 10

'My dad has brown hair and eyes that are blue.'

Sophie, 6

'My dad is called David. He has brown hair and blue eyes and he is very tall.'

Naomi, 7

Love and Affection

'My daddy grows lots of vegetables, which Mummy makes us eat.'

David, 6

'He takes me fishing, but we never catch anything!'

Ryan, 7

'My dad tucks me up in bed at night, reads me a bedtime story and says, "God bless!" before kissing me good night.'

Sarah, 11

'My daddy gives me three pounds for pocket money which I normally spend on sweets.'

Jack, 8

'When it's raining, Dad gives us a lift to school, but most of the time he makes us walk, saying we need the fresh air.'

John, 11

'I think he looks like Tarzan.'

Trevor, 8

'Dad spends hours reading the paper, which he likes doing.'

Alex, 8½

'I love my dad because he's my dad.'

Jane, 7

'My dad has very long legs which are hairy and my friends call him 'Daddy Long Legs'.

Tim, 8

'He pretends that he's a vampire.'

Simon, 7

'I never know what to buy Dad for his birthday. Mums are easy to buy things for as they like more things.'

Sarah, 10

'My friends call him 'Mr Mumbles'.'

Ken, 8

'I like it when Dad plays tennis and badminton with me on summer evenings because Mum says, "Come in," but Dad says, "Just a little longer."

Victoria, 8 3/4

'I think my dad is kind. He's kind because he takes me swimming.'

Sophie, 6

'I like my dad. He lets me do what I want.'

Natasha, 7

'I like my dad because he spends money on me.'

Daniel, 12

'He teases me and makes me laugh.'

Ryan, 7

'I love it when Dad and I are watching TV together because we will lay on the sofa together and he'll cuddle. Although we always have to watch what he wants which is normally sport - football mainly.'

Emma, 12

'Sometimes when he kisses me, it's like being kissed by a hedgehog.'
Maria, 7

'He's perfect just the way he is.'
Donovan, 7

HERO

'Dad is brilliant as he can always fix things when they need fixing, like my bike.'

Rebecca, 9

'My dad goes out to work every day and earns lots of money.'

Robert, 6

'Mummy says that Daddy is much better at doing the washing up than she is.'

Thomas, 8

'I like the way my dad knows all the answers to my homework. And he can play the piano.'

Jane, 11

'Dad makes great bread.'

Paul, 13

'He's very good at DIY. He can make benches, chairs and things like that.'

Daniel, 12

'He's a great cook. And he always does the washing up afterwards.'

Alistair, 11

'There is nothing I would change about my dad - he's great.'

Emily, 15

'I don't want him to go away when he works.'

Sophie, 6

'I would not like to change anything about him, because I like him the way he is.'

Naomi, 7

'I have a maths tutor and I do homework, and if I'm stuck Dad shouts at me because I got the answers wrong. I know he only does this because he loves me.'

Joanna, 8 1/2

'I love my dad because I can talk to him about anything: he listens and gives me advice without being judgmental.'

Amber, 17

'My dad is always teasing my mum.'

Dan, 9

'He's always quite affectionate towards me. He goes to the park and plays games when I ask him to.'

Joe, 11

'Dad tries to tidy my bedroom as a way of being helpful but I can't find anything afterwards.'

Clio, 16

'I love my dad when he buys me presents.'

Thomas, 10

'Dad drives our car very fast.'

David, 6

'He cuddles me and always kisses me before I go out somewhere.'

Suzy, 8

'My daddy is bigger, taller and fatter than all the other daddies in my road, and could beat them up.'

David, 6

'He's considerate and does things for us. He takes us out and buys us things.'

Emily, 15

'He's more laid back about things than Mum is.'

Sarah, 14

'When I am down, he'll cook my favourite food to cheer me up. He also brings me tea in the mornings and shouts when it's time to get up and get ready.'

Clara, 15

'Dad does funny impressions of people in the street. He waves his arms about in the air, puts on a funny voice and screws up his face. It makes me laugh.'

John, 12

'He shows me that he loves me by grabbing me and tickling me and throwing me about.'

Jane, 11

'I'd like him to do less work and more DIY because that makes him happy.'

Amber, 17

'My dad means everthing to me since Mum died. When I was younger he explained that Mum had gone to heaven and could still see us and was looking after us up there. It was comforting to know this.'

Emma, 14

Embarrassment

'Dad sings and dances to *Top of the Pops* in front of the gas fire'.
>Ruth, 12

'He snores in bed. It's noisy!'
>Robert, 6

'Daddy kissed a woman - YUCK!'

Paul, 7

'His farts are really funny. They are big and smelly.'

Simian, 7

'When cooking supper, he just seems to burn everything.'

Jamie, 12

'One time Dad got very drunk and it was embarrassing because he kept falling over.'

Paula, 10

'He gets really stressed out by little things.'

Craig, 12

'He whistles loudly in the street and plays with the change in his pocket.'

Amber, 14

'He embarrasses me in public by making a fuss over nothing, although unlike Mum, he doesn't nag.'

Thomas, 10

'He takes me to watch Manchester United and shouts and screams very loudly when they score a goal.'

Jamie, 12

'When I grow up I don't want to be a dad because you have to keep giving your children money.'

Charlie, 7

'Why can't Daddy shave under his arms and legs like Mummy does?'

Sarah, 8

'His taste in music is very old. It's all 60's stuff and he's always singing along to the songs in the car - very loudly.'

Daniel, 12

'I would change the way he uses talcum powder because he gets it everywhere, which drives Mum and I bonkers.'

Sally, 8½

DISCIPLINE

'He can be a bit bossy at times, although he will listen to my opinions (but not always do what I tell him to do).'

Alistair, 11

'I don't like it when he tells us off.'
                                          Sophie, 6

'Dad tells me off when I have friends round. He complains we make too much noise.'
                                          Jane, 11

'He shouts at me in the supermarket, often because I want him to buy something that he thinks is a waste of money. But he will always buy the food I want after a little nagging from me.'

Tamsin, 10

'There are not many things I don't like about my dad, but when he smacks me, I don't like him.'

Naomi, 7

'When I get in a bad mood with my dad, I stop talking to him - well try to. But I can normally only hold out for a few hours because every time my dad catches my eye he smiles and makes me smile too. Then I just start laughing and we begin talking again.'

Louise, 14

THE END